I0712166

Seraphic

ISBN: 9798883661210

Printed in the USA

Cover and Interior Designs by Gabyriella Foster

Disclaimer: The poems in this collection are a work of fiction. Any resemblance to actual events, locales, or persons, living or dead, is entirely coincidental.

Designed by Gabyriella Foster

Published Independently by Amazon KDP

THIS BOOK IS DEDICATED TO MY BEST FRIEND AND MY LOVE.
IT'S ALWAYS YOU FOR ME.

SERAPHIC

A POETRY COLLECTION

GABYRIELLA FOSTER

SERAPHIC

INK & AFFECTION

HEART'S CROSSROADS

LOVE'S SWIFT CASCADE

TEMPTATION'S TOLL

OCEANIC SERENADE

DESIRE'S DISSONACE

HIDDEN HARMONY

PLAYER'S CHARADE

UNDER THE STARS

SPRINGTIME RENDEVOUZ

PANDEMIC

QUARANTINE

UNFORSEEN BLESSINGS

SOLITARY

FATE'S INTERVENTION

BABY STEPS

PAST & PRESENT

JANUARY JOY

STRANGERS & SOULMATES

INK & AFFECTION

In the hushed corridors of academic grace,
A shy girl navigates her new workplace.
Among the whispers of students' dreams,
She glimpses a guy, more than what he seems.

Her demeanor veils a quiet storm,
A tempest of feelings, slowly taking form.
Playing hard to get, a delicate charade,
Internally, his presence makes her unafraid.

Through the labyrinth of papers and plans,
She conceals the bloom of affection that spans.
Yet, in every meeting, in every shared task,
He becomes the question she dares not ask.

In the realm of student life's steady hum,
She weaves a narrative, her heartstrings strum.
He, the protagonist in her workday rhyme,
His laughter, the melody that transcends time.

She wears a cloak of mystery, a shy ballet,
Yet within, emotions fervently betray.
In the cadence of projects and shared delight,
He's the color palette in her black-and-white.

College students, fumbling through the plot,
In the book of life, a chapter not forgot.
She yearns for dialogues beyond the mundane,
For in his presence, a novel begins to gain.

A theater of glances, a play of restraint,
In the stage of student life, love paints.
He, the understated hero she secretly keeps,
A treasure trove of moments in the heart's keeps.

As days unfold like pages in a book,
In the quiet spaces where emotions look,
A shy girl discovers a love unfurled,
In the rhythm of workday, in the student world.

———————— ♥ ————————

HEART'S CROSSROADS

In the office glow, a complex ballet,
She's entwined in a story, emotions at play.
Her heart's a canvas, a portrait unclear,
Caught in the crossroads of love and fear.

In the dance of deadlines, she wears a guise,
In her world of routine, a tempest lies.
A relationship tethered, fraying at the seam,
As echoes of neglect invade her dream.

Her partner, a chapter she thought she knew,
Yet the plot twists, emotions anew.
In the corridors of student life's lore,
Another presence knocks on her heart's door.

A guy at work, a silent symphony,
His presence, a question in her melody.
She plays the part, wears her commitment like gold,
Yet in secret glances, a new story is told.

He showers her with the warmth she craves,
In his kindness, she finds the love she braves.
Conflicted heart, torn between two shores,
One she knows well, the other, yet explores.

————————— ♥ —————————

Her partner's affection, a dwindling flame,
While the office guy kindles an untamed aim.
She cares for both, in a love's paradox,
Caught in the crossfire, love's uncharted docks.

In the stillness of night, contemplation's veil,
She wonders if love could set sail.
Between duty and desire, a precarious truce,
In the battleground of hearts, the girl's confused.

To stay in the known, or venture into the new,
A dilemma that in her silent moments brew.
In her eyes, a storm of conflicting views,
As she contemplates the love she could lose.

In the quiet turmoil of choices untold,
She wonders if hearts can be consoled.
A shy girl caught in love's intricate brew,
Yearning for a compass, a love that's true.

———————— ♥ ————————

LOVE'S SWIFT CASCADE

In the dance of risks, a daring flight,
She embraced love, bathed in its light.
A shy girl, now bold in passion's glow,
A tale of heartbeats that freely flow.

He, a melody in her life's sweet song,
In his laughter, a place where she belongs.
She fell, not slowly, but in a swift cascade,
A love story in the quietude, gently laid.

His presence, a canvas of colors bright,
Made her heart dance in the soft twilight.
Smiles and laughter, a harmonious blend,
With him, her soul found a faithful friend.

Falling fast, a leap into the unknown,
In his warmth, her heart had grown.
Days off blurred in the light of his gaze,
She lingered, basking in love's warm maze.

Work became more than a routine chore,
A shared adventure, a love to explore.
She'd visit on days when rest called her name,
Just to be near, in love's gentle flame.

———————— ♥ ————————

In his eyes, a refuge, a haven secure,
A connection deep, a love so pure.
He made her feel seen, a rare delight,
In his presence, she found peace at night.

He was the smile in her morning sun,
A love story where two hearts had begun.
Though risks entwined their tale's decree,
She felt alive, loved, and completely free.

In the labyrinth of love, she took her chance,
A shy girl now in a daring romance.
He, the reason for her heart's soft hymn,
A love that made her feel truly seen.

TEMPTATION'S TOLL

In the quiet of the night, she bears the weight,
A burden heavy, a heart in debate.
A tale of infidelity, a love astray,
In the tangled web of secrets, she lost her way.

She danced with danger, in passion's embrace,
Sought solace in a new love's grace.
Her boyfriend's heart, a casualty unseen,
In the shadows of deceit, love turned mean.

She held onto lies, like fragile threads,
As her heart wandered where new love treads.
Promises made, intentions feigned,
In her heart, the truth remained.

She thought to spare him, a Christmas of cheer,
But the truth, like a specter, drew near.
Her betrayal unveiled, in the holiday's glow,
A love once cherished, now lost in woe.

Shame floods her soul, regret cuts deep,
In the silence of her conscience, she weeps.
She longs for forgiveness, redemption's embrace,
Yet her heart clings to the new love's trace.

A tangled web of desires untamed,
In the aftermath of love's game.
She's torn between guilt and desire's lure,
In the crucible of choices, she endures.

A girl caught in the throes of passion's sway,
In the aftermath of love's betray.
She seeks solace in the arms of the new,
Yet in her heart, the old love's residue.

She yearns for absolution, a chance to mend,
In the broken fragments of love's end.
A journey fraught with shame and regret,
In the saga of love's intricate fret.

But amidst the chaos, a truth remains clear,
In the labyrinth of her heart's frontier.
She sought love's refuge, in pursuit of light,
A girl lost in the shadows, seeking respite.

OCEANIC SERENADE

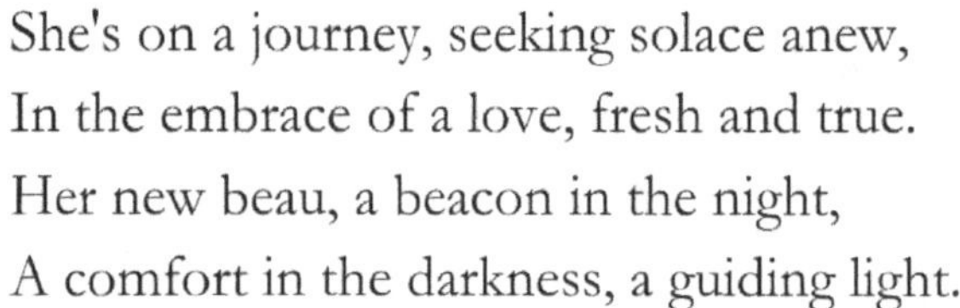

In the quiet of her room, she sits alone,
A heart adrift, in a world of its own.
Leaving behind a love once held dear,
In the wake of parting, a silent tear.

She's on a journey, seeking solace anew,
In the embrace of a love, fresh and true.
Her new beau, a beacon in the night,
A comfort in the darkness, a guiding light.

He's gone away, to a tropic isle fair,
Leaving her heart in tender care.
Yet through the distance, their love still thrives,
In the echoes of their voices, love survives.

Every day and night, she calls his name,
Seeking solace in his words, devoid of blame.
They speak for hours, hearts intertwined,
In the sanctuary of love's embrace, they find.

Her ex, a memory, a ghost from the past,
In the shadow of regret, their love didn't last.
She feels the pang of guilt, the weight of shame,
Yet in her heart, she knows it's not the same.

Their love had withered, like petals in the breeze,
In the garden of their past, memories freeze.
She doesn't want him back, that's clear,
Yet the pain of hurting him, she holds dear.

In the tropic island's embrace, her new love lies,
His absence a bittersweet compromise.
Through the miles, their hearts remain entwined,
In the symphony of love, a melody defined.

She finds solace in his voice, a sanctuary true,
In the whispers of affection, love's residue.
Her heart may ache for the one she left behind,
But in the arms of her new love, peace she'll find.

——————— ♥ ———————

DESIRE'S DISSONANCE

In the circle of her friends, a cautionary tale,
Whispers of warning, in love's gale.
They knew her heart, they knew her ways,
Yet in the shadows of her choices, doubt sways.

She confides in them, her heart laid bare,
The truth of her betrayal, a burden to bear.
Their words, like arrows, pierce her soul,
In the echoes of their caution, she finds no control.

"If they cheat with you, they'll cheat on you," they say,
A mantra of wisdom, in love's fragile fray.
They disapprove, yet their love remains,
In the backdrop of her choices, their friendship strains.

Torn between loyalty and desire's flame,
In the crucible of love, she's caught in shame.
They caution her, they plead with her heart,
Yet in the allure of passion, they drift apart.

She grows distant from them, drawn to his side,
In the sanctuary of his love, she seeks to hide.
Their disapproval lingers, like a shadow in her mind,
Yet in his arms, solace she finds.

——————— ♥ ———————

Her heart torn between loyalty and love's sweet embrace,
In the tangled web of choices, she finds her place.
She knows the risks, yet she takes the chance,
In the dance of love, she finds her trance.

Her friends may disapprove, their caution clear,
Yet in the depths of her heart, love draws near.
She's torn between their wisdom and passion's call,
In the quiet of her soul, she stands tall.

For love is a journey, both tender and true,
In the labyrinth of emotions, she finds her hue.
She may drift from her friends, yet love remains,
In the tapestry of her heart, its melody sustains.

———————— ♥ ————————

HIDDEN HARMONY

In the whispers of the office, a silent tale,
Two hearts entwined, their love unveiled.
Secret glances, clandestine smiles,
In the dance of secrecy, love beguiles.

They deny the rumors, the suspicions that rise,
Yet in their togetherness, love defies.
Taking breaks in sync, leaving side by side,
In the shadows of secrecy, their love can't hide.

Every payday, a ritual they keep,
At the local joint, where memories leap.
Shakes and burgers, a simple delight,
In the simplicity of love, they find respite.

She looks forward to those stolen moments,
In his presence, her heart's torment.
Free from judgment, free from fear,
In his embrace, love draws near.

They don't need grand gestures, or words profound,
For in his presence, her heart is crowned.
Feeling loved, feeling cherished and adored,
In the whispers of love, she finds her reward.

Their secret bond, a sanctuary true,
In the office's hustle, love breaks through.
Though suspicions linger, they stand tall,
For in each other's arms, they have it all.

In the simplicity of moments shared,
Their love blooms, in whispers declared.
A secret love, a cherished flame,
In the quiet of their hearts, love reigns.

———————— ♥ ————————

PLAYERS CHARADE

In the whispers of her colleagues' tongue,
Doubt arises, like shadows hung.
They speak of him, a player's guise,
In the echo of their words, doubt flies.

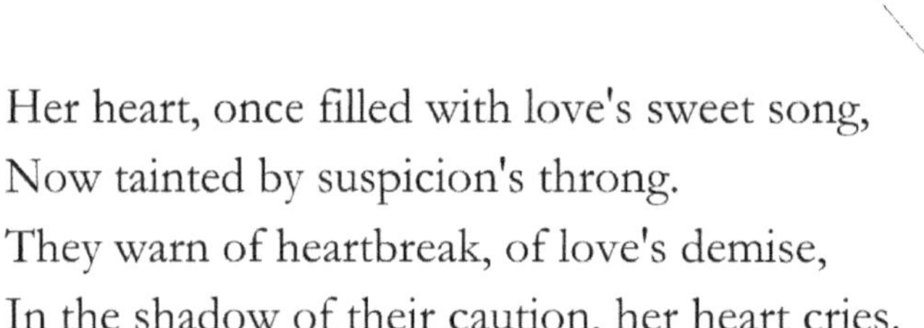

Her heart, once filled with love's sweet song,
Now tainted by suspicion's throng.
They warn of heartbreak, of love's demise,
In the shadow of their caution, her heart cries.

She watches as girls flaunt their charms,
Before him, in love's fleeting arms.
Yet he remains unmoved, untouched by their sway,
In the dance of doubt, her heart in disarray.

Is this the love she risked it all to find,
In the tangled web of hearts unkind?
Her heart still loves him, yet doubt creeps in,
In the cacophony of others' sin.

————————— ♥ —————————

She took a risk, she ventured far,
Yet now she questions who you are.
Is he the love she's been searching for,
Or a mirage, in love's tempest's roar?

Her heart is torn, between love and doubt,
In the maze of uncertainty, she seeks a route.
She longs for clarity, for truth to shine,
In the shadows of doubt, her heart's confine.

Yet amidst the whispers, love still lingers,
In the quiet moments, her heart still lingers.
She'll trust in love, despite the fear,
For in the end, love's truth will appear.

UNDER THE STARS

Underneath the city lights, they roam,
On the bus ride home, together they're drawn.
She finds solace in his presence, so near,
In the rhythm of the journey, she holds him dear.

Late-night adventures, to the beach they stray,
In the moon's soft glow, their worries sway.
Hand in hand, they walk the shore,
In the silence of the night, their hearts soar.

She spends the night at his house, safe and warm,
As her mother seeks love, her own storm.
In his arms, she finds her sanctuary,
In the haven of his love, she's free.

He's the anchor in her tumultuous sea,
In his embrace, she finds her plea.
Amidst the chaos of life's grand scheme,
He's the constant in her wandering dream.

––––––––––– ♥ –––––––––––

Every night, on the bus ride home,
In his presence, she's never alone.
He's the beacon in her darkest night,
In his love, everything feels right.

In the tapestry of life, he's her thread,
In his arms, she finds her stead.
He's the only thing that matters, it's true,
In her world, he's her sky, her ocean, her blue.

SPRINGTIME RENDEZVOUS

In the springtime's gentle embrace, they roam,
To a place where love finds its home.
With their friend in tow, a secret they keep,
In the depths of their hearts, their love runs deep.

A weekend getaway, a house to themselves,
In the sanctuary of love's secret shelves.
Amongst friends, yet in their own world they reside,
In the quiet moments, love's whispers coincide.

Amidst the laughter of their friends around,
They steal glances, in love's silent sound.
When no one watches, they dance in the night,
In the rhythm of love, their hearts take flight.

In the hush of the evening, they find solace,
In the warmth of each other's embrace.
Cuddled close, beneath the starry sky,
In the depths of their love, they lie.

_______________ ♥ _______________

Their friend knows their secret, yet stays discrete,
In the sanctum of trust, they find their beat.
Amongst the group, yet alone they find,
In the quiet moments, their love intertwined.

As the weekend fades into memory's embrace,
In the echoes of love, they find their place.
With their friend by their side, their love prevails,
In the sanctuary of friendship's sails.

——————— ♥ ———————

 # PANDEMIC

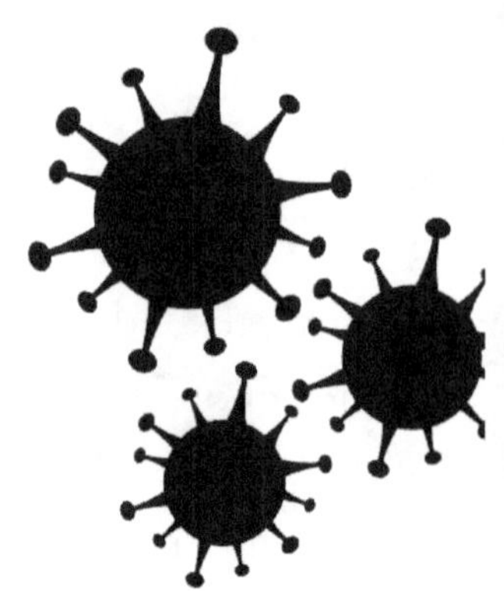

In the whispers of caution, a friend's concern,
Warnings of a virus, the world to discern.
People laugh it off, in ignorance's sway,
Unaware of the storm, heading their way.

Days pass by, in the rhythm of routine,
Yet in the shadows, a pandemic unseen.
The world carries on, unaware of the tide,
As the virus spreads far and wide.

Then comes the email, a message grim,
"Don't come back to work," the world's hymn.
Quarantine looms, a world on hold,
In the face of uncertainty, fear takes hold.

They find themselves caught, in the midst of the storm,
In the silence of quarantine, they're reborn.
No more bustling streets, no more crowded halls,
In the quiet of isolation, the world stalls.

————— ♥ —————

QUARANTINE

In the stillness of the night, he comes for her,
Amidst the silence, their love does stir.
Though supposed to be apart, they find a way,
In the cloak of darkness, they steal away.

Late-night rendezvous, in the quiet streets,
He picks her up, their hearts do meet.
Off to the local wing spot, they go,
In the warmth of each other's glow.

They laugh and talk, amidst the night's embrace,
In the haven of love, they find their place.
Though the world may seem different, uncertain and strange,
In the sanctuary of their love, nothing's changed.

They hold onto normalcy, amidst the storm,
In the wings and laughter, their hearts do warm.
For though the world may be in disarray,
In the embrace of love, they find their way.

Through the trials and tribulations, they stand strong,
In the face of uncertainty, their love prolong.
For even in the darkest of nights, they see,
In each other's arms, they're meant to be.

———————— ♥ ————————

UNFORSEEN BLESSINGS

In a new place, an hour away,
She visits him every weekend to stay.
But on her first visit, something's amiss,
Sick all day, a feeling of abyss.

She fears the virus, its deadly toll,
In the midst of a pandemic's hold.
But a friend suggests, a different route,
A pregnancy test, a different truth.

Positive it reads, her world in a spin,
How could this happen, how to begin?
In the midst of a pandemic's sway,
How to raise a baby, she's afraid to say.

Overwhelmed by fear, by doubt and dread,
In the silence of her heart, she's led.
How to navigate this new unknown,
In the world's chaos, she feels alone.

SOLITARY

Alone in the silence, she bears the weight,
In the darkness of night, her fears relate.
Pregnant and alone, over an hour away,
In the hospital, she spends her days.

Complications arise, each week a new fight,
In the depths of despair, she loses sight.
The pandemic's grip, a cruel twist of fate,
No one by her side, to alleviate.

Her love suggests abortion, a thought so bleak,
But the mere notion makes her feel weak.
How can she bear to end a life so dear,
In her heart, love for her baby is clear.

Yet the hospital stays, the depression's toll,
How long can she bear, her heart's heavy soul?
Alone in the silence, she cries in the night,
Longing for solace, for a guiding light.

————— ♥ —————

FATE'S INTERVENTION

In the depths of despair, she stands alone,
At her lowest ebb, her heart a stone.
Agreeing to go, to the clinic she's bound,
To end a life, her heart's profound.

But fate intervenes, with a cruel twist,
Denied the abortion, her heart a fist.
No ID in hand, the deed delayed,
By the time she gets one, the choice will fade.

The future now clear, she's bound to be,
A mother-to-be, with no decree.
In the midst of her turmoil, sickness strikes,
To the hospital she's taken, her heart dislikes.

On her birthday, in the hospital she lies,
Messages of joy, masking her cries.
People reach out, with wishes sincere,
Unaware of her plight, her burden severe.

———————— ♥ ————————

She has to act happy, as if all is well,
In the depths of her despair, her heart a shell.
But behind the facade, her tears do fall,
In the quiet of her room, her heart does call.

Alone in the hospital, her heart does ache,
In the midst of her sorrow, her soul does break.
Yet amidst the darkness, a glimmer of light,
In the love of her baby, she finds her might.

BABY STEPS

In the quiet of acceptance, her journey begins,
With each passing day, a new chapter spins.
Her birthday hospital visit, a turning tide,
As she embraces motherhood, fear subsides.

No more long hospital stays, once she accepts,
The baby's arrival, her heart intercepts.
Pregnancy becomes a joy, little by little,
As she prepares for motherhood's riddle.

Buying clothes, toys, necessities abound,
In the warmth of anticipation, she's found.
Telling friends and family, her heart alight,
In the glow of excitement, everything's right.

But in the depths of her heart, a fear resides,
Of how her love feels, of what he decides.
Scared he'll abandon them, leave them alone,
In the face of uncertainty, her heart a stone.

She doesn't know if it's over, if he'll stay,
In the silence of her fears, she finds her sway.
Yet amidst the doubt, a glimmer of hope,
In the bond with her baby, she finds her scope

———————— ♥ ————————

PAST & PRESENT

At the baby shower, joy fills the air,
Friends and family gathered, love to share.
But amidst the laughter, an unexpected sight,
Her ex-boyfriend, a ghost from the past night.

He stands there silent, no words to say,
A reminder of a different yesterday.
She feels guilt gnawing, deep inside,
For the heart she broke, the tears she cried.

Yet his presence there, it irks her so,
An unwelcome guest at her baby's show.
No gift in hand, no words to share,
Just a silent reminder of a love affair.

But amidst the discomfort, love prevails,
In the arms of her loved ones, her heart sails.
Surrounded by support, by those who care,
In their embrace, her burdens she'll share.

Though guilt may linger, and annoyance too,
In the love of her family, her heart finds its hue.
For amidst the complexities of love and past,
In the present moment, her love will last.

JANUARY JOY

In the chill of early January, a day serene,
The moment arrives, a dream unseen.
She brings forth life, a miracle so pure,
In the arms of her love, their bond secure.

A boy they welcome, with tender care,
In the hush of the room, love's whispers rare.
She watches her love, with their child in his arms,
His eyes alight with love's gentle charms.

In the glow of the moment, hope takes flight,
In the promise of tomorrow, everything's bright.
For in the depths of their love, they find their way,
In the embrace of their son, a new day.

With each breath he takes, their hearts do swell,
In the wonder of parenthood, they do dwell.
Though challenges may come, they'll face them together,
In the warmth of their love, they'll weather.

For in the birth of their son, they find their light,
In the depths of their love, everything's right.
Their future ahead, a path unknown,
But with love as their guide, they'll call it home.

———————— ♥ ————————

STRANGERS & SOULMATES

In the passage of time, almost five years gone by,
Through the highs and lows, beneath the sky.
Challenges arose, like storms in the night,
But love prevailed, in its steadfast light.

They met as strangers, in a world so vast,
But fate had woven, a love that would last.
Through trials and tribulations, they held on tight,
In the depths of their love, everything's right.

Through moments of joy, and moments of tears,
In the ebb and flow of the passing years.
They faced the storms, hand in hand,
With unwavering love, they took a stand.

Through laughter and sorrow, they journeyed on,
In the tapestry of life, their love shone.
For almost five years, they've weathered the storm,
In the warmth of their love, they found their form.

So here's to the girl and the guy, who stood tall,
Through it all, they never did fall.
For love's enduring flame, forever will burn,
As they continue on, in each other's turn.